I0820418

CLOUD COMPUTING

Published in 2025 by **Cheriton Children's Books**
1 Bank Drive West, Shrewsbury, Shropshire, SY3 9DJ

First Edition

Author: Kelly Roberts
Designer: Paul Myerscough
Editor: Jennifer Sanderson
Proofreader: Amy Strauss
Consultant: David Hawksett, BSc

Picture credits: Cover: Shutterstock/3d_man (t), Shutterstock/Kaspars Grinvalds (c), Shutterstock/SeventyFour (bl), Shutterstock/Ground Picture (br). Inside: p4: Shutterstock/Blackboard, p5: Shutterstock/Arnav Pratap Singh, p6: Flickr/Mike McBey, p7: Shutterstock/Rawpixel.com, p8: Shutterstock/Ievgen Gluzhetsky, p9: Shutterstock/BublikHaus, p10: Shutterstock/Sevennine_79, p11: Shutterstock/Rawpixel.com, p12b: Shutterstock/SeventyFour, p12t: Shutterstock/Ikoimages, p13l: Wikimedia Commons/Stansfield PL, p13r: Wikimedia Commons/Steve Jurvetson, p14: Shutterstock/Ryan DeBerardinis, p15: Shutterstock/Zef Art, p16: Shutterstock/Ground Picture, p17: Shutterstock/Summit Art Creations, p18: Shutterstock/Fizkes, p19: Wikimedia Commons/Dr. Frank Gaeth, p20: Shutterstock/Ground Picture, p21: Shutterstock/Lucky Business, p22: Shutterstock/3d Man, p23: Shutterstock/Gorodenkoff, p25bl: Flickr/Financial Times, p25br: Flickr/TechCrunch, p25t: Shutterstock/Alexey Boldin, p26: Shutterstock/Rafapress, p27: Shutterstock/Fizkes, p28: Shutterstock/Prostock Studio, p29: Wikimedia Commons/Brian Smale, p30: Shutterstock/Fizkes, p31: Shutterstock/Ground Picture, p32: Shutterstock/Ground Picture, p33: Shutterstock/Monticello, p34: Shutterstock/Rawpixel.com, p35b: Shutterstock/Frederic Legrand/COMEO, p35t: Shutterstock/Yalcin Sonat, p36: Shutterstock/Aodaodaodaod, p37b: Flickr/Magnus Höij, p37t: Shutterstock/Tada Images, p38: Shutterstock/Panuwat Phimpha, p39b: Wikimedia Commons/GS200, p39t: Shutterstock/Yakub88, p40: Shutterstock/Tsingha25, p41: Shutterstock/Photosince, p42: Shutterstock/DC Studio, p43: Shutterstock/Aiman Khair, p44: Shutterstock/Rawpixel.com, p45: Shutterstock/Gorodenkoff.

Printed in China

Please visit our website,
www.cheritonchildrensbooks.com
to see more of our high-quality books.

CONTENTS

CHAPTER 1

THE CLOUD COMPUTING STORY

Every day, more than 1 billion people around the world use computer apps such as Dropbox, Gmail, iCloud, and Spotify. When people use these Internet-based services, they are making use of cloud computing, perhaps without knowing it! Cloud computing is about using personal computers (PCs), laptops, smartphones, and other Internet-enabled devices in new, exciting ways to unlock the power of the Internet.

What Is the Cloud?

In the world of information technology, cloud computing means providing services such as email and file storage to many users across a computer network. This is quite different from traditional desktop computing in which the apps people use and documents that they create are stored on a PC at home or in an IT suite at school.

The rise of the Internet along with increasing computer power has made the cloud possible. Emails, shopping, personal data storage, and smart devices are all powered by the cloud.

Today, anyone with a smartphone can record videos or broadcast live on social media. Once uploaded, files are stored in the cloud via massive data centers.

Workspace and Personal Cloud

For most businesses, the cloud is a private network within the company. The cloud is the internal network of servers and the services they provide. The server feeds into every computer terminal within the business so workers can access what they need. For most people, cloud computing is all the services they can plug into over the Internet. It places the apps and files that we need on the Internet, making them available anywhere in the world with a wireless connection and an Internet-enabled device.

Using the Cloud

Cloud computing covers many different web-based apps that people use every day. The apps include web mail such as Gmail and Outlook, file storage systems such as Dropbox, social networking sites such as TikTok, and music clouds such as iTunes and Spotify. In this book we'll discover more about the technology that makes cloud computing work. We'll also explore the history of cloud computing, how is has changed your world, and the brilliant scientists behind this incredible invention.

HOW HIGH-TECH CHANGED THE WORLD

Before cloud computing became common, people stored their documents on their PCs. They could not share files unless they saved them to separate devices. Today, we can store documents, music, and our photographs in the cloud —our files are accessible on all our devices, not just our PCs, and sharing them is as simple as sending a link or inputting a password. Thanks to cloud computing, we can also contact friends and family via email and social networking sites. Cloud computing has made the world a smaller, more accessible place.

Running Programs

Cloud computing has forever changed the way everyone uses computers—instead of running all the programs on a computer at home, cloud computing uses remote machines in the "cloud" to run them for you. But this would not be possible without the development of personal computing and an English mathematician named Charles Babbage (1791–1871), who began designing the first computer in the 1830s. His steam-powered machine, the Analytical Engine, could add up tables of numbers.

Getting Bigger

In 1943, British mathematician Alan Turing (1912–1954) built Colossus, the first fully electronic computer. Colossus was designed to crack secret codes used by the Germans during World War II (1939–1945). Three years later, US physicists John Atansoff (1903–1995), John Mauchly (1907–1980), and Presper Eckert (1919–1995) built the Electronic Numerical Integrator and Calculator (ENIAC). The enormous machine weighed an incredible 30 tons (27 mt).

Smaller and Smaller

Computers became much smaller following the invention of the transistor in 1947. Scientists realized they could build all the electronic parts of a computer on one small circuit board, called an integrated circuit (IC). This led to the invention of the microprocessor, or microchip. Microchips made computers much smaller and more powerful.

Colossus was huge. Since its invention, computers have become so powerful that they no longer take up a whole room!

The invention of the laptop allowed people to work away from the office, and eventually connect to the Internet from public spaces.

The Computer Boom

During the 1970s, the first PCs were invented. Computer experts developed operating systems for people to use the new PCs, such as Microsoft's MS-DOS and Apple's Graphical User Interface (GUI). At the same time, they developed programs such as word processors and spreadsheets.

HIGH-TECH HISTORY

The first laptop computers appeared in the 1980s. The Grid Compass, launched in 1982, was the first computer that opened and closed like a clam. It was not very powerful and had a $8,000 to $10,000 price tag, but its size and portability meant it was used by astronauts on the Space Shuttle as well as by the US military. Apple's iMac revolutionized desktop computing when it appeared in the 1990s. In the early 2000s, PCs were powerful enough to take advantage of the rise of broadband Internet connections. Today, computers exist in many different forms, from netbooks and smartphones to tablets and smart televisions.

Today, floppy disks have been replaced by USB sticks, memory cards, and external hard drives for portable storage.

Linking the Computers

The computing revolution meant that more people owned computers. The next logical step was making PCs "talk" to each other so people could use them to share data and communicate with each other. Before the computing revolution, people had to physically share computers to access the data on another computer. So, computer experts came up with inventions, such as floppy disks, to make sharing data much easier and more practical for people.

Early PCs relied on floppy disks to transfer data and install software. These were overtaken by optical disks, which held far more data and accessed it much more quickly.

Early Internet?

In 1962, a computer scientist named Joseph Licklider (1915–1990) came up with the idea of a computer network while working at the Advanced Research Projects Agency (ARPA). He called his idea the Intergalactic Computer Network. It worked using a new communication protocol called packet switching, which involved transferring messages as neat packets of data. Eventually, this developed into the Advanced Research Projects Agency Network (ARPANET for short). ARPANET paved the way for the Internet.

Connecting Cables

In 1973, Robert Metcalfe developed Ethernet. Ethernet could be used to connect many computers and other devices within a building. Ethernet worked by using cables running from machine to machine in a local area network (LAN). Computer networks can be much bigger than a LAN. Metropolitan area networks (MANs) connect computers in whole towns or cities using telephone lines. Bigger still are wide area networks (WANs), which can cover almost any geographical area. The Internet is an example of a WAN.

HOW HIGH-TECH CHANGED THE WORLD

Today, people in offices and at home connect to devices, such as printers, using wireless networking (Wi-Fi) technology. Instead of using cables, Wi-Fi uses radio waves to transmit data through the network. Before Wi-Fi, every device connected to the Internet via a cable, usually connected to a router, which could take several cable connections at once. Today, wireless routers are still connected to the Internet via a cable, but they broadcast their Internet connection in a short-range "bubble." A phone or computer with Wi-Fi can connect with the bubble as if connected by a cable. Many other devices, such as security cameras, smart lights, and smart speakers also connect to a network using Wi-Fi.

Many cafés and restaurants have their own Wi-Fi router, which broadcasts a bubble big enough to cover the venue.

A Global Network

The Internet is a WAN that covers the entire planet. In reality, it is a global "network of networks" through which people can share ideas and information, and communicate with each other. The Internet started in the early 1960s, when scientists from the US Department of Defense (DoD) set up ARPANET. They invented the language that allowed computers to share data and communicate, making the Internet possible.

Adding Computers

At first, the network consisted of just three computers based at universities in the United States. But, by 1984, more than 1,000 computers were connected to ARPANET. In 1986, the National Science Foundation (NSF) set up five supercomputing centers to speed up the connections to ARPANET. Within a year, the number of computers connected to the network had grown to 10,000. Eventually, the new National Science Foundation Network (NSFNET) replaced ARPANET to become the backbone of the Internet in the United States.

Going Global

By the 1990s, the Internet had expanded throughout the world. Companies called Internet Service Providers (ISPs) started to sell Internet access to individual users. Then, in 1991, British computer scientist Sir Tim Berners-Lee developed the World Wide Web (WWW). This world-changing invention allowed people to use web pages stored on servers connected to the Internet.

The WWW made using the Internet much more user-friendly and it grew rapidly, with many countries, home users, and organizations becoming connected.

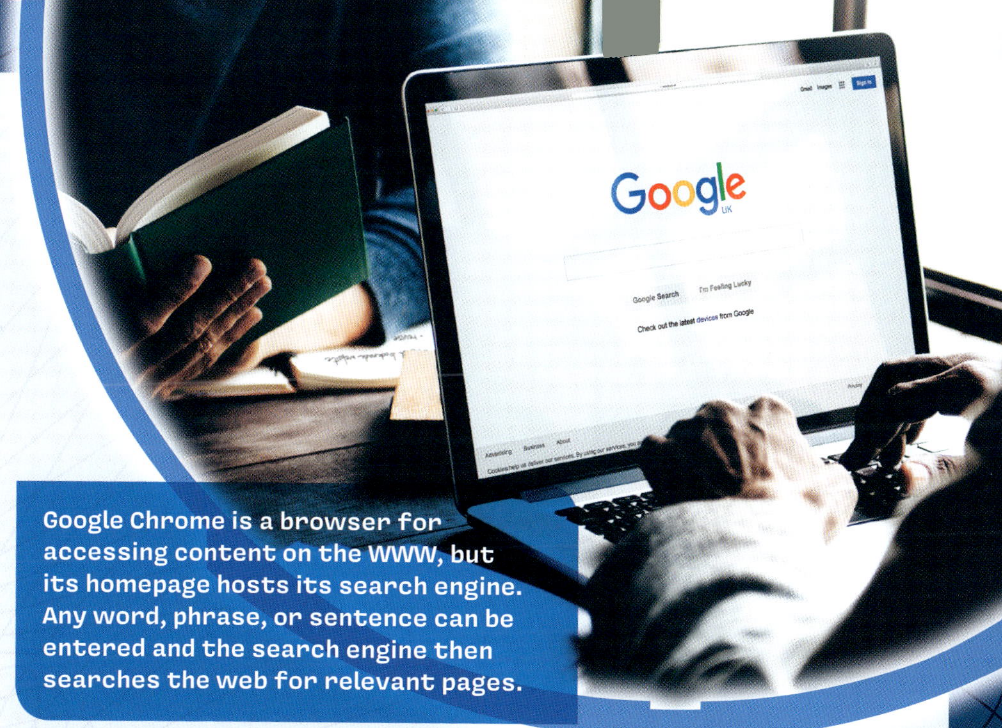

Google Chrome is a browser for accessing content on the WWW, but its homepage hosts its search engine. Any word, phrase, or sentence can be entered and the search engine then searches the web for relevant pages.

The Internet Is Born

In 1995, the NSF handed over management of the Internet to the ever-growing number of ISPs. Today, the Internet connects people in almost all countries around the world. It helps people keep up to date with the news, play games, buy groceries or theater tickets, and chat with family and friends who are both nearby and far away.

HIGH-TECH HISTORY

In the early 1990s, a team at the National Center for Supercomputing Applications (NCSA) at the University of Illinois developed the Mosaic browser. It was one of the very first browsers that made the growing WWW available to everyone. It made online content more user-friendly, allowing text and images to be easily viewed. It paved the way for more advanced browsers such as Netscape and Internet Explorer, and our modern browsers such as Google Chrome, Safari, Firefox, and Opera.

Some cloud-computing systems, such as the music cloud Spotify, have their own apps that provide users with access to the cloud services. Users can listen to music whenever and wherever they like.

Back and Front

Cloud computing is divided into the front (user) end and the back (system) end. The front and back ends communicate with each other through a computer network, which is most often the Internet.

At the Front

The front end of a cloud computing system is the part that the computer user actually uses. It includes the user's personal computer and/or computer network and the interface software. Interface software is needed to access the cloud computing system. Many cloud services, such as web-based email (Gmail and Outlook) use Internet browsers such as Microsoft Edge or Google Chrome.

At the Back

The back end is the "cloud" section of the system. This includes all the various computers, servers, and file storage systems that make up the cloud of computing services. Cloud services include almost every type of app, from email and file storage to music and video games. In most cases, each app will have its own dedicated server.

Cloud computing is so called because all the applications and information exist on a cloud of web servers, like this one, rather than on the user's workstation.

The Middleware

The front and back end of a cloud computing system use computer software, called middleware, to "speak" to each other. Middleware acts as a bridge between different technologies so that they can communicate with each other. Without this one smart computer software, computer scientists would have to build a data-exchange system for every single piece of connecting software. A central server administers the cloud system and follows a specific set of rules, called protocols, to ensure everything runs smoothly.

Sergey Brin

Larry Page

HIGH-TECH STARS WHO CHANGED THE WORLD

LARRY PAGE AND SERGEY BRIN

Larry Page and Sergey Brin were both PhD students at Stanford University, California, when they founded Google. In 1998, the pair decided to move their server from a student dorm room to somewhere larger. They rented a garage big enough to accommodate two cars, for five months, before finally renting a proper office. Google started as a search engine, then a browser, and then a wide array of cloud services including maps, email, office apps, and online storage. Google's current headquarters cover 2 million square feet (185,000 sq m). Its search engine home page is the top-visited website in the world.

CHAPTER 2

THE INTERNET AND CLOUD COMPUTING

The Internet is the backbone of most cloud computing systems. The only thing you need to run cloud services is the interface software, which is usually a web browser. When scientists started the Internet, they needed to allow computers to share data in a way that made sense to everyone. They set up rules so that all the computers on the network followed the same set of instructions. This important set of rules became known as the TCP/IP suite—the Transmission Control Protocol (TCP) and Internet Protocol (IP).

Smaller Packets

Using the TCP/IP suite, any information to be transferred through the network is broken down into smaller parts called "packets." Each packet is given an IP address, which is a special number for the destination computer. As the data packet passes through the computer network toward its destination, file servers "switch" the packet along the way.

The network is like a busy road. A group of ten people (packets) cannot fit in one car, so they split up. Each person will travel in a different vehicle and maybe along different lanes, but they will end up at the same destination.

The IP address of the packet tells the servers which way to switch the packet. Each time a server switches the packet, it gives the packet a "wrapper." This tells us which and how many servers handled the packet on its journey. A file sent from the United States to Australia can be switched up to 15 times. This means 15 file servers were needed to deliver the packet to its destination. Data packets from the same computer file do not always travel along the same route but they all end up at the same destination.

HOW HIGH-TECH CHANGED THE WORLD

Packet switching arose from an idea for a process called "hot potato routing." Paul Baran (1926–2011) worked at the RAND Corporation, a Californian research institute. In 1959, during the Cold War, US military leaders worried that a nuclear attack would disrupt their communications. Baran took on the job of designing a communications system that could survive such an attack. Hot potato routing was his solution, and his system allowed for communications to be sent via many routes, avoiding any that were damaged. Packet switching made ARPANET possible.

The threat of nuclear attack and the need to design a communications system that could operate in that event was the inspiration for packet switching.

Network Chains

Different organizations work together to exchange information over the Internet. Most people pay an ISP to use Internet services. In turn, the ISP pays bigger organizations higher up the chain. The Internet uses many different ISPs to route information. Consumers are at the bottom of the chain. They include individual computer users and businesses, which pay a fee to an ISP to connect to the Internet. The ISP is the first step in the routing hierarchy. All the ISPs together make up what is known as a Tier 3 network.

Free Sharing

All the ISPs on the Tier 3 network pay to connect to one or more ISPs on the Tier 2 network. ISPs on the Tier 2 network are Internet providers. All the ISPs on a Tier 2 network pay to connect to a Tier 1 network. Some also use "peering." Peering means the ISPs on the Tier 2 network share each other's Internet traffic for free. Peering opens up more connections to the Internet. It also allows for more data sharing and improves the performance of each ISP.

The infrastructure of the ISPs includes the reliable connectivity and security needed to to shop, book tickets, and manage our bank accounts online.

ISPs in China serve around 20 percent of all the world's Internet users. With more than 1 billion users, China has more people connected to the Internet than any other country. India comes second, with around 900 million users.

Huge Company Sharing

Tier 1 networks are made up of enormous telecommunications companies, all of which share Internet traffic with each other without paying for the service. Historically, ARPANET and later NSFNET made up the Tier 1 network. Big telecommunications companies took over when the US government opened up the Internet to the public in 1995.

HIGH-TECH HISTORY

NSFNET was created in order to link five new supercomputer centers in US universities. It began operations in 1986, using the TCP and IP, but could only send data at 56 kilobits per second. More universities joined the network and by 1987 it became clear that the demand for data was greater than the amount that the network could provide. Soon new connections were added that could carry data at 1.5 megabits per second. Data traffic congestion meant the amount of data carried by the early Internet had to keep growing, and the volume continues to grow today.

Today, billions of people regularly use Internet services such as the WWW and email. The Internet allows us to keep in touch with family and friends on video calls, make new friends on social networking sites, and shop and play games online.

The Web Is Born

In the past, people needed a desktop computer, a modem, and a telephone line to use the Internet. Today, using a wireless connection to devices such as tablets, laptops, and smartphones, you can access the Internet from just about anywhere in the world.

Following Protocols

Before the WWW was created, most Internet users were computer experts. Most people could not understand the complex language and tools needed to share data on the Internet. In 1991, new ways to transfer information through the Internet were created. These protocols, which are still used today, are: HTTP (HyperText Transfer Protocol), HTML (Hypertext Markup Language), and the URL (Uniform Resource Locator) system.

Using Protocols

HTTP, along with several other standards, became known as the W3 protocols, named for the W3 Consortium that was set up to oversee the development of the WWW. Today, anyone can use the Internet to access and share data and their thoughts.

People use web browsers to find and read web pages using the HTTP protocol. File Transfer Protocol (FTP) clients allow people to share and download files. Email programs use the Post Office Protocol (POP) and Simple Mail Transfer Protocol (SMTP). The Network News Transfer Protocol (NNTP) is used to exchange messages, called articles or posts, between users on Internet discussion forums.

Internet on the Move

Mobile access is one of the fastest-growing areas of the Internet. Anyone with a smartphone and a wireless connection can access services such as email and the WWW. Cloud computing is an important part of this mobile revolution because it allows people to access important files and services wherever they are.

HIGH-TECH STARS WHO CHANGED THE WORLD

SIR TIM BERNERS-LEE

Sir Tim Berners-Lee is the British computer scientist who invented HTML, HTTP, the URL system, and the WWW. In 1980, he was working at CERN, the international particle accelerator laboratory on the France-Switzerland border, when he came up with the idea of hypertext. By 1989, CERN was the largest European section of the Internet, and Tim realized that he could combine his hypertext idea with TCP and DNS (Domain Name System) to create the WWW.

CHAPTER 3

HOW THE CLOUD WORKS

Most people are familiar with the front end of a cloud computing service. This is usually a website or an app that they use to access files, play music, or post a status update. The back end is the invisible part you cannot see. This is where all the processing takes place and where the cloud exists.

Servers in the Cloud

Imagine a data center humming with racks of machines called servers. When you log on to a cloud service, you are connecting to these powerful computers. Some servers give commands to allow you to do specific tasks, such as log on to an account or play a music file. Other servers are simply massive storage drives that hold important files. Together, these servers become a cloud of resources.

Connecting Computers

A server is any computer and the software on the computer that is used to manage resources on a network. In a LAN in an office, there may be a file server to store important files. Any computer on the office network can access the files through the file server.

Apple and Google phones automatically upload photos to the cloud where they are stored and can be shared.

Office computer workstations all connect to the Internet through the office's central server, which acts as a miniature cloud for its users. The server controls all of the security, encryption, and data storage, which would otherwise need to be managed separately for each computer.

Servers for the Web

The Internet relies on web servers to deliver web pages to computers connected to the web. To do this, the computer uses a computer program called a browser, which sends a request to the web server in the form of a URL. A URL consists of three main parts: the HTTP protocol, the server name, and the file name. Look at the following URL: https://www.un.org/en/events-and-news

- HTTP is the HyperText Transfer Protocol—the language that the browser uses to find and speak to the web server
- un.org/en identifies the United Nations (UN) homepage in English
- events-and-news is where files in the form of news articles are available

HOW HIGH-TECH CHANGED THE WORLD

The servers that support the cloud are usually housed in data centers. The amount of computing power in these facilities means they use a lot of electricity and generate a lot of waste heat. Scientists have found smart ways to make data centers more environmentally friendly. In Switzerland, an IBM data center uses its waste heat to warm a local swimming pool. Another data center in Finland uses its waste energy to provide hundreds of homes with heat.

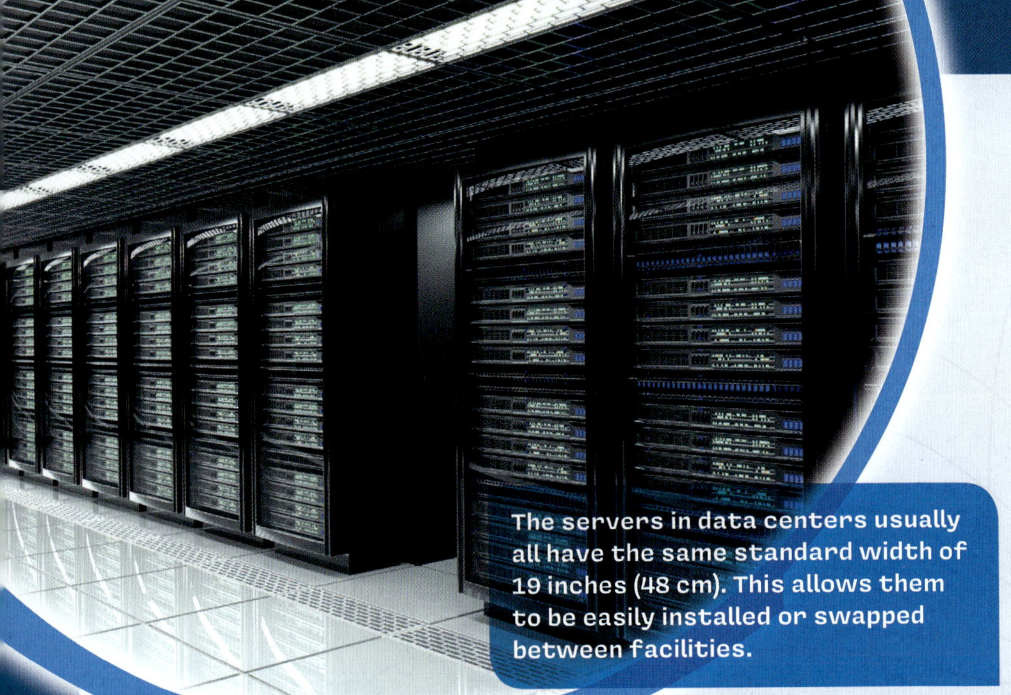

The servers in data centers usually all have the same standard width of 19 inches (48 cm). This allows them to be easily installed or swapped between facilities.

Dealing with Users

Some cloud services have millions of registered users, so they need a lot of servers to do many different jobs. One way to manage this is to create "virtual" servers, which increase the power of the service so it can handle many tasks, without needing to buy extra computer hardware.

Using Virtual Servers

Most servers usually do just one particular task. This streamlines the computer network and makes it easier to solve problems, but as a computer network grows, more and more servers are needed to carry out an increasing number of tasks. Additional servers take up room and generate a lot of heat. "Virtualization" can solve these expensive problems.

Having a Host

Virtualization involves using one computer to "host" a virtual server. Instead of functioning as part of the computer, the virtual server behaves like a completely separate device. For example, a computer running the Microsoft Windows operating system could be used to host a virtual server that runs another operating system, such as Linux. The computer is called the host machine, and the virtual server is the guest. While the host computer runs all the Windows apps, the virtual server can run the apps for the Linux system. The two systems do different jobs on the same computer.

Benefits of Virtual Servers

Virtual servers can run several tasks on one physical machine. Since fewer machines are needed, using a virtual server saves energy and avoids the need to buy more expensive hardware. Virtualization also reduces maintenance costs—it is much quicker and easier to update just one computer running multiple virtual servers than it is to maintain several individual computers.

Virtual servers are commonly used by businesses to run many virtual machines on just one physical server. Using virtual servers also makes it easier to back up, copy, and restore data and files.

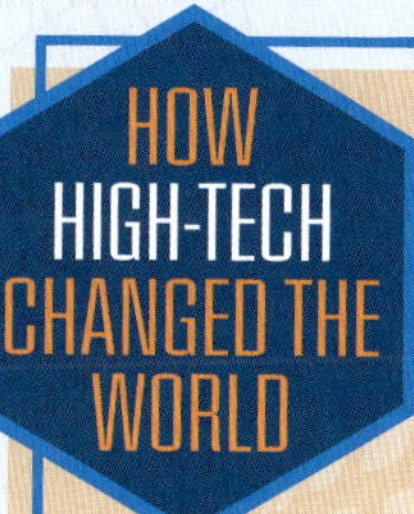

Computer scientists working at IBM created the world's first virtual computer in the 1960s. The experimental system was built on the IBM 7044 computer, which hosted multiple 7044 guest machines. Called the M44, this was proposed as a research project, and it evolved from the need for time-sharing on computers. The idea of virtual computing was that multiple users could be using one computer at the same time, even though each user had the impression that only they were using the computer.

One Server, Many Tasks

Multitenancy is one of the buzz words of cloud computing. It means one server carries out all the different tasks needed to run the service, and serves every single customer. In an office, one server handles requests from all the computers on the network. In the cloud, a single server may serve millions of customers. One physical server would not be able to deal with all these requests alone. As a result, many cloud systems use multitenancy. This means there are several clones (identical servers) to handle all the traffic. Every one of these servers is exactly the same. Users can connect to any one of the cloned machines and it will be able to deal with their request.

With multitenancy, multiple users can access the same app at the same time with no disruption to service.

What Are the Benefits?

Many popular cloud services such as Dropbox, iCloud, Google Apps, and Netsuite work using the multitenancy model of cloud computing. One of the main benefits of multitenancy cloud computing is that if one server fails, all the information is safely stored on all the other clones, so users can access information all the time.

Infinite Speed

Multitenancy increases the speed of cloud services, regardless of how many people are using them. Imagine a web mail service such as Gmail with millions of users. Multitenancy ensures that the service can handle all the traffic if everyone sent an email at the same time. Servers called load balancers handle the peaks and troughs of demand. These servers direct all the messages to the right place as soon as they are sent. This ensures a speedy service for everyone.

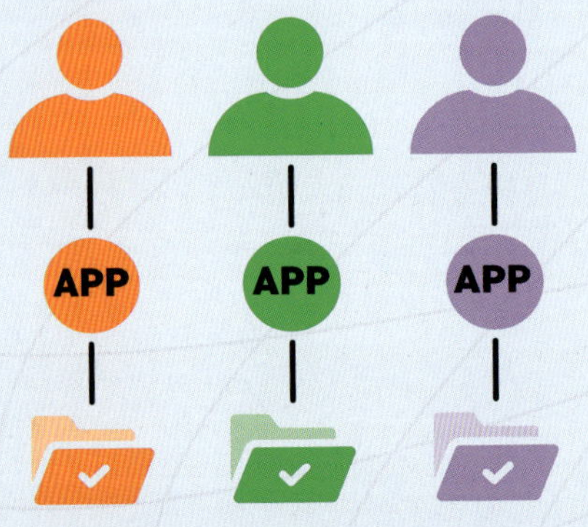

without multitenancy

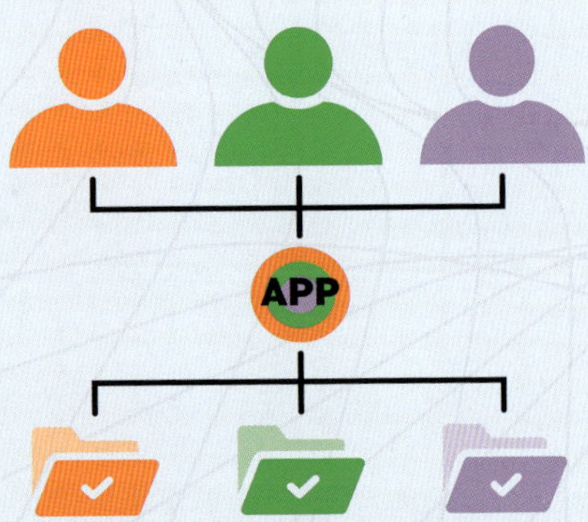

with multitenancy

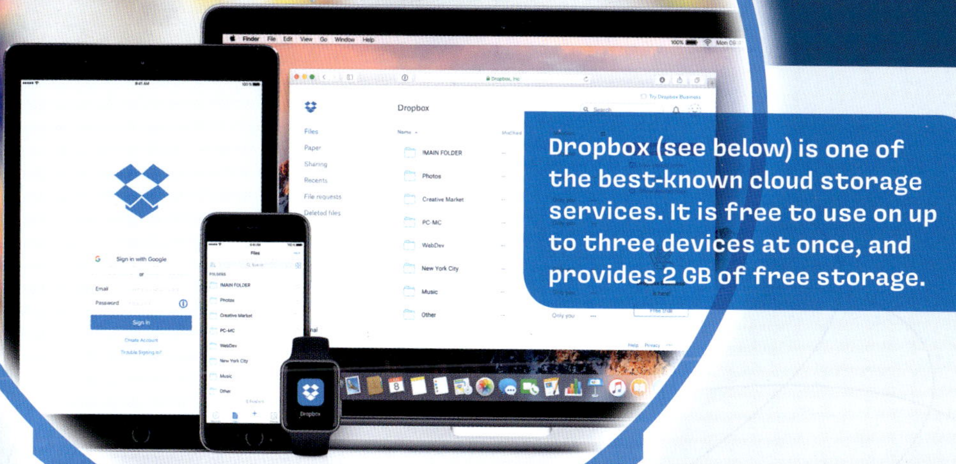

Dropbox (see below) is one of the best-known cloud storage services. It is free to use on up to three devices at once, and provides 2 GB of free storage.

Arash Ferdowsi

Drew Houston

HIGH-TECH STARS WHO CHANGED THE WORLD

DREW HOUSTON AND ARASH FERDOWSI

In 2007, MIT student Drew Houston was traveling when he realized he had forgotten to bring his USB flash drive. This gave him the idea that people should be able to access their files on any device and from any location. If files and data were stored in the cloud, people would not need to carry flash drives and they would no longer be needed. The following year Houston and his fellow student Arash Ferdowsi launched Dropbox, an online file storage site that expanded to include file sharing and other features. Today, Dropbox has more than 700 million users around the world.

When the Walt Disney Company launched its Disney+ streaming service in 2019, they decided to use Amazon Web Services rather than build their own data centers. This has allowed the channel to grow to around 150 million users without Disney needing to buy its own servers for streaming.

Cloud Services

Cloud service providers offer three basic services: Software as a Service (SaaS), Platform as a Service (PaaS), and Infrastructure as a Service (IaaS). SaaS delivers one app to several customers. The provider owns the app and uses the Internet to deliver the service through a web browser, a dedicated app, or both. The customer benefits because there is no software to purchase, install, and update—the service provider does all of this for them. One example of a cloud-based SaaS app is Google's Gmail. This webmail service replaces traditional desktop email clients such as Microsoft's Outlook Express.

Sending Apps

PaaS allows customers to send apps to people via the Internet. In this case, the customer is a business that develops its own customized apps. The service provider provides hardware, software, and hosting services to deliver web-based apps. An example of a cloud platform is Microsoft Azure, which hosts cloud services for many customers.

Hosting Cloud Services

Some companies, such as Amazon and Google, hire out their computing resources to host cloud services. They provide all the hardware, such as servers, networking, and a data center, so other companies can provide the service. This is called Infrastructure as a Service (IaaS). One example is Netflix, which streams movies and television programs to customers using Amazon's cloud platform.

Newer Types

Two new types of cloud computing include Network as a Service (NaaS) and Communication as a Service (CaaS). NaaS delivers network services, such as servers and routing equipment, to customers over the Internet.

HOW HIGH-TECH CHANGED THE WORLD

In 2011, Microsoft launched Office 365 as a subscription service based in the cloud. Its aim was to move its customers away from buying software to paying an annual fee to access its office programs using a web browser. Today, the service is called Microsoft 365, and it has ended the need to have separate software for spreadsheets, word processors, and other office apps installed on computers. By keeping files in the cloud, users can access them anywhere on any device, including smartphones. Such cloud computing services have completely changed how we store and access our data.

CaaS provides cloud-based services such as phone calls and video conferencing.

Having their company infrastructure in the cloud has made it possible for businesses and other organizations to keep their employees' remote access secure.

Different Ways for Different Customers

Cloud computing can be offered to different customers in different ways. These are called deployment models and they control who is allowed to use the cloud services. There are three main deployment models: public clouds, private clouds, and hybrid clouds.

Quick and Easy Access for the Public

Public clouds give people quick access to the resources needed to use a cloud service. The service provider manages the hardware, software, and supporting infrastructure, and offers cloud services such as apps and file storage to the general public. Many public clouds are free, although some charge a fee. Most public clouds offer people access to the Internet via a browser or app interface.

Private Clouds

Some companies run private cloud services that limit the cloud service to one company. Private clouds usually use the PaaS model (see page 26). The company develops the software and then uses it through an external service provider. In this way, companies can deliver specific software to employees and clients without the infrastructure costs. Private clouds companies also have control over the service, which keeps data safe.

Both Public and Private

Hybrid clouds are based on private clouds. However, they also take advantage of the benefits of public clouds. Companies may use private clouds for applications and sensitive data, but still rely on the benefits of public cloud services, such as hardware and software support.

The Ultimate Cloud

One exciting new idea in cloud computing is to combine all the different cloud services into one huge cloud network, called the "Intercloud." This global "cloud of clouds" would be similar to the Internet, the global "network of networks" on which most cloud services are based.

HIGH-TECH STARS WHO CHANGED THE WORLD

SATYA NADELLA

Satya Nadella became Chief Executive of Microsoft in 2014. He was previously the company's head of cloud computing. Under his leadership Microsoft has focused more on cloud computing than ever before. Its cloud computing services and platform are known as Microsoft Azure, which includes data storage, networking, databases, computing power, and artificial intelligence (AI). Azure is now one of the top-three cloud computing platforms, along with Amazon Web Services and Google Cloud Platform. It is supported by a global network of data centers.

CHAPTER 4

BETTER CONNECTED

Cloud computing provides access to email and all our important documents from anywhere, from any device, and at any time. Cloud computing is all about being connected. It is the perfect partner to our mobile lives.

Email Access

Web mail services allow people to send and receive emails through a website. The website can be accessed using a web browser. A POP account allows messages to be sent and received using an email client, or program, such as Thunderbird. Every time you check your email, the account downloads new messages from the server into the email program.

Internet Message Access Protocol (IMAP) accounts also allow people to send and receive emails using an email program. However, in these accounts, the messages are stored in the cloud rather than by the email program.

What's Good about Web Mail?

Web mail offers a number of advantages over desktop email clients. For example, web mail services offer so much online storage that you can leave all your emails and attachments in the cloud. You can then access them from anywhere and download them to an email program on your PC.

What's Not Good?

One of the downsides of web mail is that you will have to see advertisements when viewing your messages on the web. Although most web mail services are currently free of charge, there is always the chance that you might have to start paying for them in the future.

HOW HIGH-TECH CHANGED THE WORLD

The Internet has also provided new ways of communicating with people through cloud services that offer phone calls and video conferencing over the Internet. Two of the most popular is Skype, which was launched in 2003, and Zoom, which saw huge growth during the Covid-19 pandemic when school lessons were held online. Both services offer free voice and video calls for users and can be used on smartphones, PCs, and tablets.

Interactive features make teaching and learning more productive and fun when using apps such as Zoom. Breakout rooms, chat boxes, voting tools, and interactive whiteboards can all be used to keep students involved.

Storing in the Cloud

Many people struggle to find enough storage space to store all their digital photos, MP3 files, and video clips. In the past, people stored these important files on external hard drives, compact discs, and flash devices. Cloud storage is now a very popular alternative.

Storing Your Data

There are many different ways that you can store important documents in the cloud. They are all available anywhere that you can connect to the Internet. Hosting companies store the files on remote servers in large data centers. People can access their data using an app or through a regular web browser.

Microsoft's Storage Solution

Today, OneDrive is one of the most popular cloud-based storage solutions. This service is free to anyone with a Microsoft account. A PC's operating system creates an icon of OneDrive on your desktop or in your apps list. All you need to do is copy the files that you want to store in the cloud. The PC then synchronizes all the files in the OneDrive on your PC to the cloud's web servers. OneDrive also allows users to synchronize files onto more than one computer. This means you can work on a document at school and an up-to-date version of the file will be waiting on your PC at home. OneDrive also has a public folder, so users can share files that are too big to be sent as email attachments.

Any information that is stored in the cloud is vulnerable to unauthorized access. Fortunately, most cloud services now use techniques, such as password protection, to ensure the information stays private.

Google Workspace

Gmail

Drive

Meet

Calendar

Chat

Jamboard

Docs

Sheets

Slides

Keep

Sites

Forms

Google Workspace is completely based in the cloud so all files can be accessed from anywhere on any device with an Internet connection.

Synching Data

With Dropbox, users create a special folder on each device they own, and the Dropbox service synchronizes it so the folder that appears is the same on every device, whether that is a computer, smartphone, laptop, or tablet. Users can also upload files using a web browser, or use an app to gain access to the service.

HOW HIGH-TECH CHANGED THE WORLD

In 2012, Google joined the list of technology companies offering cloud storage when it launched Google Drive. Google's set of online office tools, include its online word processor—Google Docs —and Google Sheets, a spreadsheet application. Google's online tools not only allow file sharing, but also let many people at once work on a shared file such as a spreadsheet or slide show.

The Cloud and Social Networking

Social networking sites have changed the way people use the Internet. These popular sites are helping people stay in touch, make new friends, post comments, upload photos, and much more. All these sites are forms of cloud storage.

YouTube introduced live streaming in 2013 for users with at least 1,000 subscribers. Now anyone with just 100 subscribers can live-stream from their phone with 4K video quality.

Big Social Hits

Facebook and Instagram are two of the most popular social networking sites. Facebook has been around since 2004 and already boasts more than 2 billion daily users worldwide. Instagram came later in 2010 and has more than 1 billion users.

Sending a Tweet

X, formerly known as Twitter, allows users to send messages called "tweets" to tell other X users what they are thinking or doing. X is an open site, so you can follow any other user. When someone whom you are following posts a tweet, their message appears in your X feed.

Friends in the Cloud

Social media sites are excellent types of cloud computing services. Sites such as Facebook, Instagram, and X, allow people to develop real relationships within the virtual world of the Internet. People can keep in touch with family and friends using messaging systems, chat forums, and blogging tools, which can be used to post "status updates" and send out invitations to events. Sites also allow users to upload photos and tag people who feature in the images. All the information people post on their profiles is stored in the cloud so it can be accessed whenever they want.

Elon Musk is an active user of X and regularly answers questions and responds to comments. He often tweets updates on other major projects such as his SpaceX space program and Tesla automobiles.

HIGH-TECH HISTORY

Twitter was launched in 2006 as a social networking site that allowed users to post "tweets," which were messages of 140 characters or fewer. By 2012, Twitter had more than 100 million users who, between them, were posting 340 million tweets each day. PayPal founder Elon Musk bought Twitter in 2022 for $44 billion. In 2023, Musk changed the name from Twitter to X. Today, the site has more than 500 million users around the world. Today's tweets are no longer limited to 140 characters and can be up to 280 characters. For those who pay a subscription fee, their tweets can be up to 4,000 characters.

Elon Musk

Music in the Cloud

Cloud computing has changed the way people listen to music. In the past, to listen to music, compact discs and, later, MP3 files were played. Cloud music services use computer servers connected to the Internet to let people access a huge library of digital music files.

A Library at Your Fingertips

Some music clouds, such as Pandora, are like personalized radio stations. Users create a profile and build up a library of music. Pandora then streams music over the Internet to match their music tastes. You can approve or reject the songs that Pandora selects, and the service automatically revises the playlist. Music clouds such as Spotify offer users more control over the music they hear. Users can search through Spotify's library of music, adding specific songs to make up personalized playlists of their favorite music.

Your Own Music

iTunes works in a different way. Users can upload their own digital music files and the service stores the files in an online music library. Users can then play the music from the website or using the service's desktop or smartphone app. iTunes also allows people to purchase new music and add the digital files to their playlists.

Limited Space

Music clouds that work as a file storage service usually limit the number of songs you can save in your online library. For example, iTunes allows you to upload 100,000 songs but albums bought from the iTunes Store do not count against this limit.

Listening to music from the cloud works best when a phone is connected to the Internet with Wi-Fi. But in open spaces away from Wi-Fi, a phone can still stream music using its own 3G, 4G, or 5G cell phone connection.

Spotify's library of more than 70 million tracks is available in over 180 countries.

Paying for a Service

Most music clouds have a version that you can try for free. They offer basic accounts with the minimum storage space and may include advertisements between songs. Premium accounts offer extra services, such as a larger music library and no advertisements, but you must pay for them.

HIGH-TECH STARS WHO CHANGED THE WORLD

DANIEL EK

Swedish entrepreneur Daniel Ek is the chief executive and cofounder of Spotify. In 2002, the illegal music sharing site Napster was shut down, and Daniel realized that the best way forward was a site that allowed music downloads and paid the artists for their work. Spotify was launched in 2008, and now has more than 380 million active users who can either pay for a subscription or use it for free, but with advertisements included.

CHAPTER 5

THE GOOD AND BAD IN THE CLOUD

Cloud computing has its advantages and disadvantages. When you use cloud services such as web mail and social networks, you have to balance the benefits against the risks. There are many different reasons why so many people are moving toward cloud computing. One of the main benefits is ease of access. Many people rely on cloud services instead of a desktop computer to access apps and important files. Cloud services work using the Internet, which is available almost anywhere in the world at any time.

Cheap and Easy

Cloud computing reduces the need for costly computer equipment and all the hardware that goes with it. You need just a simple Internet-enabled device, such as a smartphone or tablet, and a Wi-Fi or cell phone network connection. The service provider pays for all the costly hardware, software licenses, maintenance, and IT support.

Saving Space

Hosting servers takes up a lot of space. Some companies rent rooms to store all this equipment because they do not have enough space on site. Cloud computing now gives users the option of storing the data in a remote site. Remote data centers also offer added benefits, such as security and server backups.

Free Wi-Fi is usually available in airports, shopping malls, and even hospitals. It allows us to be online almost constantly, even in a place with poor or no cell phone connection.

Ed Sheeran's X Tour saw a record-breaking 8.9 million tickets sold for 260 shows around the world between 2017 and 2019. Cloud-based services enable huge global events like this and ensure all tickets go to the correct owners—even when using different ticketing systems in different countries.

Adding Power

Cloud services offer increased server capacity to handle a lot of traffic. Imagine a ticketing company that sells tickets for a popular artist. Cloud services can tap into the processing power of many computers, speeding up the ticket sales.

MARTIN COOPER

Mobile devices have been partly responsible for the evolution of cloud computing. They enabled the ability to access everything while on the move. This would not have happened without the invention of the cell phone. Engineer Martin Cooper created the first cell phone in 1973. He made the first-ever cell phone call to his rival Joel Engel (who had also been working to build a cell phone) to boast of his achievement. His phone needed a 10-hour charge to provide just 30 minutes of call time. It weighed 2.5 pounds (1.1 kg) and was nicknamed "the brick!"

The Drawbacks of the Cloud

The idea of handing over important information to a service provider to host on the Internet raises concerns. The biggest worries are privacy, security, and reliability. If you can access all your important computer files in the cloud, there is always the risk that someone else could access them, too, and use them without your knowledge. As a result, almost all cloud service providers use different authentication and authorization processes to protect data that is held in the cloud.

Password Protection

Authentication protects data using a password. Users create a password when they sign up to the service. The data itself is also encrypted, which means it is scrambled and requires an encryption key to decode. You unlock the encryption key by entering the correct password. Authorization involves giving specific users access to apps and files, which can be restricted by profile. Each user can then access only the data and apps relevant to their profile.

Biometrics are increasingly used as a safer way to secure your data than using just a password or PIN. Phones and other devices can be accessed by recognizing your face with a camera, or by reading your fingerprint on a scanner.

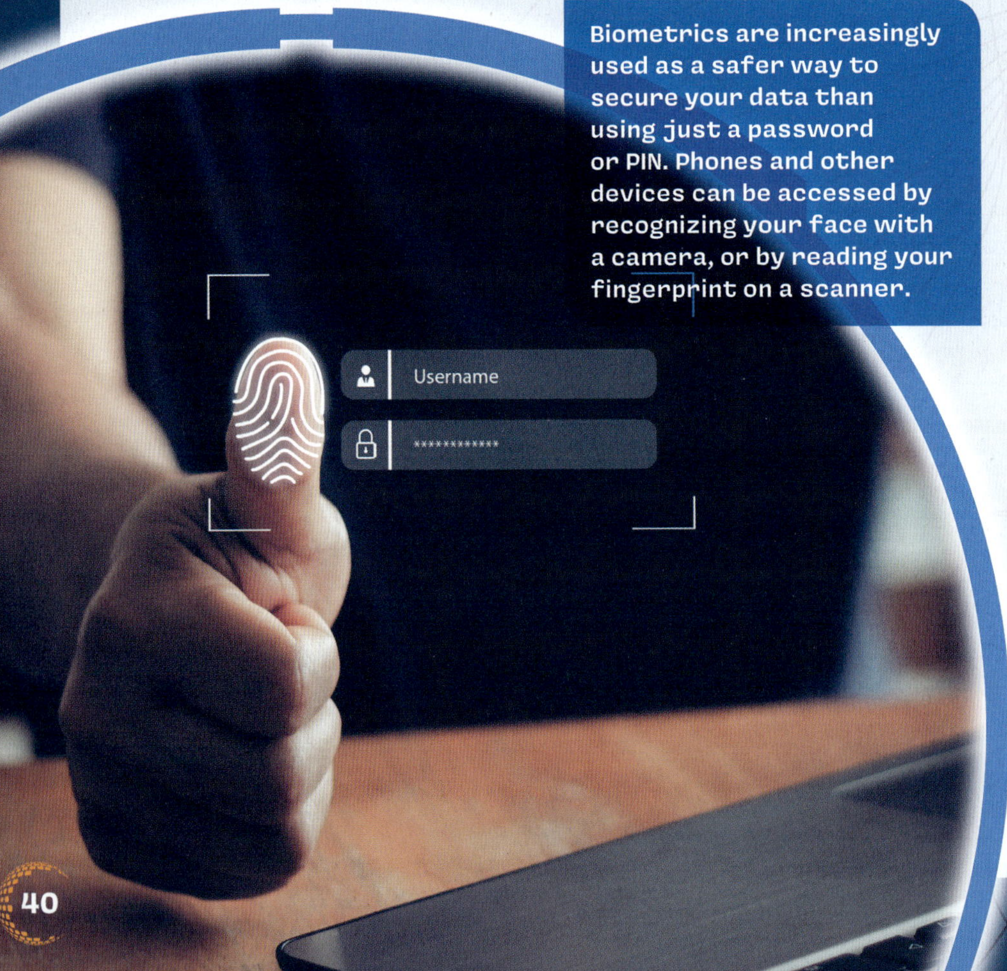

HIGH-TECH HISTORY

Amazon was founded by Jeff Bezos in 1994 as an online book store. It expanded to include movies, music, and electronics in the late 1990s. Today, you can buy anything and everything on Amazon. Its rapid expansion included its purchase of the live-streaming site Twitch in 2010. Amazon keeps its number of users a secret but it is certainly one of the largest e-commerce sites in the world.

Jeff Bezos

Is the Cloud Reliable?

Most people take cloud computing for granted, but what happens if something goes wrong? Do you want to store important data if the cloud is going to fail? Internet connections are not always reliable, and technical problems will occur from time to time. Although cloud services are more robust, outages still occur today. On December 24, 2012, Amazon cloud services went offline and were unavailable for more than 22 hours, resulting in a huge loss of cash for sites relying on Christmas revenue.

Who Owns the Data?

Another problem faced by users of cloud computing is the ownership of data. If you give another company your personal information, do you still own the data? When you sign up to cloud services, you must agree to the terms and conditions of the sites. It is important to read these legally binding documents carefully before you agree to use the services.

Online gaming became popular in the early 2000s, as more people had broadband Internet connections at home. PCs are still used by many people to play online, especially for the more complex options such as multiplayer online role-playing games.

A Cloud for Everyone

Cloud computing is not just about moving servers into a data center. It is changing the way people use computers to store data and access services such as music and social networks. Cloud computing is everywhere. These services are hidden behind the Internet so many people are not aware of the cloud, even though they rely on it to go about their work or for fun. Cloud computing is revolutionizing the way people use computers and the Internet. It is helping them tackle the challenges of computer upgrades, maintenance, and security.

Saving to the Cloud

Many people now use cloud services to store their important or meaningful information, such as photos, which take up a lot of memory. Schools, companies, and universities rely on cloud computing to store apps and libraries of information. Games such as Minecraft are also using cloud services. They allow many users to create "servers" to play with other users, making games even more interactive for the users.

Mobile Cloud Services

Although many people use Internet-enabled smartphones and other mobile devices to access cloud services on the move, there is a limit to the amount of data you can store on these devices. As a result, many services are providing mobile cloud services to fill this need.

What the Future Holds

Cloud computing may seem like the latest trend in the world of personal computing, but it is not an end in itself. Cloud computing is a helpful technology. It allows individuals and companies to achieve their goals and makes computing much easier for everyone. Cloud services such as iTunes and iCloud have come a long way in such a short space of time. Who knows what the future may hold in store?

HOW HIGH-TECH CHANGED THE WORLD

Every time we use a navigation app on our phones we are using the cloud. Google Maps was launched in 2005, providing detailed maps that could be used via a browser. In 2007, it began linking with Global Positioning System (GPS) data, showing users their exact location on a map in real time. Google Maps now also shows live traffic congestion, restaurant reviews, and three-dimensional (3-D) and satellite views. All this data is stored in the cloud in Google's own data centers and it is fed to our devices whenever we browse the map.

A smartphone's AI voice assistant can be used to input destinations and change them during a journey. A smartphone navigation app can even share your location with friends.

CONCLUSION

A HIGH-TECH FUTURE

Cloud computing has been around for many years but it seems to be the new buzz phrase in information technology. Web mail, social networking, and cloud storage are some of the most popular applications of cloud computing, and it looks like that trend will continue for some time to come.

Using the Internet

Most cloud computing systems make use of the Internet to provide their services to many users around the world. They have developed smart tools such as virtualization and multitenancy to ensure people can access the cloud from anywhere in the world at all times. Many companies now offer cloud services. They include web mail services such as Gmail and Outlook, file-sharing apps such as WeTransfer and Dropbox, social networks such as Facebook and Instagram, and music clouds such as Apple Music and Spotify.

More people are turning away from traditional desktop computers in favor of mobile computing. They are using Internet-enabled devices such as smartphones and tablets and connecting to the cloud. The future of cloud services looks set to continue.

New data centers are being built all over the world in a global network that should be resistant to a catastrophic large-scale loss of data due to a major natural disaster.

Advantages and Disadvantages

Cloud services have advantages and disadvantages. Some of the advantages include easy access, increased processing power, and reduced hardware costs. Some of the disadvantages include concerns about privacy and security, issues surrounding ownership of the data in the cloud, and also what could happen if data was lost in the event of a widespread war or a huge natural disaster.

The Next Revolution

The confidence in cloud computing is growing and more people are signing up to services such as social networks and music clouds. For public cloud users, issues such as privacy and security are now less of a concern. Businesses are also seeing the benefits of cloud computing in the form of reduced operational costs and increased processing power. Just as the Internet revolutionized computing in the 1990s, cloud computing is proving to be the next revolution.

HOW HIGH-TECH CHANGED THE WORLD

The increasing demand for cloud computing by organizations means its use will only increase. The amount of money spent each year on the infrastructure for cloud computing is now approaching $1 trillion. Security and network reliability are constantly being improved, as well as the available cloud computing power. The sharp rise in AI will drive even more growth as companies increasingly use it to remain competitive. The growing number of data centers are hungry for electricity but, in the long term, science and innovation will make them much more environmentally friendly and sustainable.

GLOSSARY

apps short for applications software: a program that tells a computer or other electronic device to do something

artificial intelligence (AI) technology that enables computers and machines to think and solve problems like humans

clients computer hardware or software that accesses a service made available by a server

Cold War a period of tension between the United States and the Soviet Union from 1945 to 1991

connectivity the capacity for connection

encryption converting data into code to prevent it being read

Global Positioning System (GPS) a network of satellites that allows people to find their position anywhere on Earth

Graphical User Interface (GUI) a visual way of interacting with a computer using icons, menus, and windows

hard drives the parts of an electronic device that store information

hardware the physical parts of a computer system, such as the machines and the cables that connect them

infrastructure the organizational structure of something

interface the point where two systems meet and interact

Internet the network of smaller computer networks that join to form a single global network

microprocessor an integrated circuit that has all the functions to control a computer

modem a device that allows computers to send and receive information over the telephone network

network a system of interconnected computers

operating systems programs that control computers

router a device that forwards data packets through a computer network

servers computers designed for a specific task, for example, storing information or running a network

software a computer application or program designed to do a specific task, for example, send email, edit photos, or record music

tablet a small, portable computer contained within a flat screen, such as an iPad

USB an acronym for Universal Serial Bus, which is a type of wired connection between devices to transmit data and power

Wi-Fi a system that allows computers and cell phones to connect to computer networks without a traditional system of cables

FIND OUT MORE

Books

Bolte, Mari. *How the Internet Will Save the World* (STEM to the Rescue). Full Tilt Press, 2022.

Peters, Jackson. *Google, the Story Behind the App* (Tech Titans). Mason Crest, 2024.

Steffens, Bradley. *Cutting Edge Internet Technology* (Cutting Edge Technology). ReferencePoint Press, 2017.

Websites

Find facts and explanations about cloud computing at:
https://azure.microsoft.com/en-us/resources/cloud-computing-dictionary/what-is-cloud-computing

Learn more about the cloud at:
https://computer.howstuffworks.com/cloud-computing/cloud-computing.htm

Discover more about Apple Computer's cloud service, iCloud, at:
www.apple.com/icloud

Publisher's note to educators and parents:
All the websites featured above have been carefully reviewed to ensure that they are suitable for students. However, many websites change often, and we cannot guarantee that a site's future contents will continue to meet our high standards of educational value. Please be advised that students should be closely monitored whenever they access the Internet.

INDEX

ABOUT THE AUTHOR

Kelly Roberts has written many children's science and technology books. In researching this book, she has learned just how much cloud computing technology has changed our working lives and our leisure time, too.